PRAYING 101

for

KIDS & TEENS

By

Dottie Randazzo

Praying 101
for
KIDS & TEENS

by

Dottie Randazzo

Creative Dreaming
6433 Topanga Cyn. Blvd.
120
Woodland Hills, CA 91303

ISBN 978-0-6151-4725-3

We should spend as much time in thanking God for his benefits as we do in asking him for them.

St. Vincent de Paul

By Dottie Randazzo

Praying 101 for Spiritual Enlightenment

Praying 101 for Kids & Teens

Praying 101 for Men

Praying 101 for Women

Praying 101 for Parents

Introduction

This book is designed for both kids and teens because, after all, there isn't much of a difference between the ages of twelve and thirteen. Now is there?

I realized a long time ago that most of us think that our prayers are not heard because we aren't getting what we want. But it's not that our prayers aren't heard; it's all in the asking. A few years ago, when a friend told me that she wanted something. I asked her if she'd said a prayer for it. She told me she didn't know how to pray.

As a child I attended both Baptist and Lutheran schools where I was taught how to memorize a few really good prayers, such as the Lord's Prayer. I was never really taught how to pray.

I know how to pray. I am not sure how I learned, but I did. All you have to do is ask my sister and she will tell you. She has often said I have a direct line to the heavens!

This book will teach you how to pray. It is your basic prayer book. I have designed a prayer for many aspects of your life. Once you have learned the key ingredients to praying you will have the tools to customize your own prayers. So let's flip the page and begin to solve the mystery of prayer.

Commonly Asked Questions

Do I need to know any special language to pray?

You do not need to know any special language. Your language and words will be understood.

Who do I pray to?

It does not matter whether you are praying to God. Our Father, The Masters of the Universe, or whomever, your prayer will be heard. Pray to the One that you believe in.

When and where should I pray?

Praying can be done anytime and anywhere. If you want to say your prayer in the morning, then that is when you should say it. If you want to say your prayer while standing in line at school, then that's when you should.

Do I have to kneel down or say my prayer out loud?

No kneeling needed. You can stand, lie down or be sitting in a park. It doesn't matter; your prayer will be heard. Your prayer does not need to be said out loud.

How do I pray?

To pray you use the little voice in your head. The same one that you hear when someone walks into the room with a weird hairdo and you hear in your head, *what was she thinking with that hair?* That's the same voice that you are going to say your prayer with. Those same voices in your head that you hear say, *I did well* or *I should not have done that.* It is almost like talking to yourself except you do it in your head. Say your prayer just like you are writing a letter; begin with "Dear____." And always end your prayer with thanks. Thanks for listening, thanks for caring, thanks for looking out for me. Gratitude goes a long way in life.

If I don't get what I am asking for, does that mean my prayer was not heard?

Not getting what you want absolutely does not mean that your prayer was not heard. We always get what we want. We may not get it when we want it. We get it when we are supposed to.

Practice in life whatever you pray for, and God will give it to you more abundantly.

Pusey

Very Important Things You Should Know

Everything happens for a reason. . If something bad happens to you, you need to look at the experience and see what you were supposed to learn from it. For example, let's say that your so-called best friend told someone a lie about you. You got hurt, felt embarrassed and betrayed by someone who you thought was your best friend. While you may have bad feelings, it is really a good thing that you found out that this person, who you thought was your best friend, really wasn't. You really wouldn't want to keep someone in your life like that. Be glad that their true colors were revealed.

Everything happens exactly when it is supposed to. This might not be when you want it to happen. For example, let's say you want to get your driver's license, really badly at the age of fifteen, but your parents won't let you. You are upset and think that they are being unrealistic. You get your driver's license when you are eighteen. If you take the time to look back, you would realize that you know so much more now at the age of eighteen than you did at the age of fifteen, and that it really was best for you to get your driver's license when you were supposed to, at the age of eighteen. And not when you wanted to at the age of fifteen.

You are doing in your life exactly what you are supposed to be doing at this exact moment. Every single moment in your life is very important and every single moment in your life affects the next moment in your life. Every person that you meet has a reason to be in your life, even if just for a brief moment. Some people come into our lives for a reason and some for a season.

Enjoy your life. You must learn to enjoy your life. Eating your breakfast in the morning is part of your life. Don't sit down and eat it fast while you are thinking of something else. This is a very bad habit to start. When you are older it will take you twice as long to fix the bad habit. Every single day is a very important day in your life. It is a day that you will never get to relive. Learn to appreciate every moment and don't take them for granted.

Pray for wisdom. Wisdom is smarts, answers, solutions and brainpower. When you ask for wisdom you ask to be aware of the right answers. Wisdom allows you to see answers when they enter your life. For example, you want a summer job and pray for one. Within a short period of time you may meet someone new who happens to offer you a summer job. You got the summer job, the answers to your prayer was delivered by someone new coming into your life. Let's say that you pray to get a great grade on an exam and then shortly someone shows you a different, better way to learn. Chances are you will get the better grade and the answer to your prayer came in the form of someone teaching you something better. Sometimes we get answers but they do not always come to us the way we think that they should and therefore we don't see the answer. We miss them because we are looking for them to be delivered our way. Answers are delivered the way that they are supposed to be delivered, not necessarily the way that we want them delivered.

Believe that your prayers are heard and will be answered. Why pray if you don't have any faith. The bible says that faith the size of a mustard seed can move a mountain. Like Wow! Have you ever seen a mustard seed? It's tiny. Don't try praying to test the system. It doesn't work. The system does not need to be tested by you.

Prayer for Toys, a Special Thing or Game

Here's how it works. Let's say you want a video game system. You pray and ask for it. Now the important part is being aware, from the moment that you have said your prayer, for the answer. A bike may magically appear if it is your birthday, or special time of the year and you have let someone know that you want it. But if it doesn't come to you that way, and you still want it, you must be open to all opportunities around you. That's why you must pray for wisdom. You want the ability to see the opportunities when they arrive. Here's one example of how your prayer could be answered; you say your prayer and then shortly after your Mom or Dad wants the garage cleaned out and offers to pay you to do it. This is an opportunity for you to make money for that bike. The answers to your prayers will show up in ways that you least expect. The key thing is to be able to see the answers.

Dear God,

I really want this thing. I pray for the wisdom to obtain it. If it isn't meant for me to have, I pray for the wisdom to understand why. Thank you for listening to me.

That's it. It's pretty simple and right to the point. No begging or bargaining needed. You may say one prayer or you may say several prayers. There is no limit on what you can ask for and receive in life.

Prayer for Better Grades in School

Dear Lord,

I pray for the wisdom to obtain better grades. I pray for the wisdom to have better concentration, better memory and fewer distractions when studying. I pray that you remove any feelings of insecurity that I possess. Thank you for taking care of me.

Prayer for Understanding my Friends

Dear God,

I pray that my friends will understand me better and that I will understand them better. I pray for the wisdom to be able to recognize my true friends from enemies. I pray for the strength to stand up for myself. I pray for the courage to not be bullied into a situation just to fit in. I pray for the wisdom to see and make the correct choices. I pray that you protect me from all evil. I pray that you remove any feelings of insecurity that I possess. Thank you for caring about me.

Prayer to Resolve Conflicts

Dear Masters of the Universe,

I pray for the wisdom to make the correct choices necessary to resolve the present conflict. I pray for the wisdom to be able to see the lesson(s) in this situation and that I am able to grow from it in a positive way. I pray for the strength and courage to help me resolve the present conflict. I pray that you protect me from all evil. I pray that you remove any feelings of insecurity that I possess. Thank you for listening to me.

Prayer for Better Communications with my Parents

Dear Goddess,

I pray for the wisdom to understand why my parents treat me the way that they do. I pray for the wisdom to resolve conflicts and add more love into our relationship. I pray for the wisdom to be able to see the lesson(s) in this situation and that I am able to grow from it in a positive way. I pray that you remove any feelings of insecurity that I possess. Thank you for taking care of me.

Prayer to Remove Pimples

Dear Higher Power,

I pray that you will give me the strength and courage to over come any humiliation that I may feel. I pray that others will not judge me because of my skin and that they will see me for the great person that I am on the inside. I pray for the wisdom to be able to see the lesson(s) in this situation and that I am able to grow from it in a positive way. I pray for the wisdom to love my body. I pray for the awareness that my body is a reflection of your creation and it is perfect in every way. I pray that you remove any feelings of insecurity that I possess. Thank you for listening to me.

Prayer for Unwanted Braces

Dear Father,

I pray for the strength and courage to over come any humiliation that I may feel by wearing braces. I pray that others will not judge me because of my braces and that they will see me for the great person that I am on the inside. I pray for the wisdom to be able to see the lesson(s) in this situation and to grow from it in a positive way. I pray for the wisdom to love my body. I pray for the awareness that my body is a reflection of your creation and it is perfect in every way. I pray that you remove any feelings of insecurity that I possess. Thank you for looking out for me.

Prayer for Unwanted Glasses

Dear Lord,

I pray for better eyesight. I pray that you will give me the strength and courage to over come any humiliation that I may feel by wearing glasses. I pray that others will not judge me because of my glasses and that they will see me for the great person that I am on the inside. I pray for the wisdom to be able to see the lesson in this situation and to grow from it in a positive way. I pray for the awareness that my body is a reflection of your creation and it is perfect in every way. I pray that you remove any feelings of insecurity that I possess. Thank you for taking care of me.

Prayer for a Lost Pet

Dear God,

I pray for the safety of my pet. I pray that my pet returns to my home. If my pet has encountered an accident, I pray that he/she is not suffering and that his/her soul is with you in Heaven. Thank you for taking care of my pet and me.

Prayer Because I am too Thin or Anorexic

Dear Masters of the Universe,

I pray for the wisdom to be able to identify bad eating habits from healthy ones. I pray that others will not judge me because of my weight and that they will see me for the great person that I am in on the inside. I pray for the wisdom to be able to see the lesson(s) in this situation and to grow from it in a positive way. I pray for the wisdom to love my body. I pray for the awareness that my body is a reflection of your creation and it is perfect in every way. I pray for good health. I pray that you remove any feelings of insecurity that I possess. Thank you for taking care of me.

Prayer to Become Popular

Dear Goddess,

I pray that others will see the sincere good person that I am. I pray that others will not judge me by my looks, talents or family background but that I will solely be accepted for the person I really am. I pray that you remove any feelings of insecurity that I possess. Thank you for looking out for me.

Prayer for Hobbies

Dear Higher Power,

I pray for the wisdom to perfect my skills and talents regarding my hobby or hobbies. I pray for the wisdom to be aware of the opportunities to become better at my hobby or hobbies. I pray for my safety and the safety of others while I am participating in my hobby or hobbies. I pray that you remove any feelings of insecurity that I possess. Thank you for listening to me.

Prayer for Dates

Dear Father,

I pray for the wisdom to date and have the right person in my life. I pray for the wisdom to see people for who they really are and not to judge them by how they look, what their talents are or what their family background is. I pray that others see me for who I really am. I pray for my safety and the safety of others on my dates. I pray for the courage to make the correct choices on my dates. I pray for the strength and courage to stand up for my beliefs and myself and not to be bullied into a bad situation just to fit in. I pray that you remove any feelings of insecurity that I possess. Thank you for looking out for me.

Prayer for Peer Pressures
(Drugs, Sex and/or Social Pressures)

Dear Lord,

I pray for the wisdom to make the correct choices. I pray for the courage to just say no. I pray for the strength to stand up for my beliefs and myself. I pray for the courage not to be bullied into a situation just to fit in. I pray for my safety and the safety of others. I pray for the wisdom to be able to see the lesson(s) in this situation and to grow from it in a positive way. I pray that you remove any feelings of insecurity that I possess. Thank you for taking care of me.

Prayer for Pregnancy

Dear God,

I pray for the wisdom to make wise choices. I pray for my health and the health of my baby. I pray for the strength and courage to stand up for my beliefs and myself and not to be bullied into a bad situation just to fit in. I pray for the wisdom to be able to see the lesson(s) in this situation and to grow from it in a positive way. I pray for the wisdom to love my body. I pray for the awareness that my body is a reflection of your creation and it is perfect in every way. I pray that you remove any feelings of insecurity that I possess. Thank you for listening to me.

Prayer for Good Judgment

Dear Masters of the Universe,

I pray for the wisdom to make the correct choices and to exercise good judgment in every area of my life. Thank you for blessing me.

Prayer for Good Health

Dear Goddess,

I pray for the wisdom to make the correct choices regarding my health and safety. Thank you for taking care of me.

Prayer for Mental Courage

Dear Higher Power,

I pray for mental strength and courage. I pray for the wisdom to make the correct choices. I pray for the strength to stand up for my beliefs. I pray for the courage not to be bullied into a bad situation just to fit in. I pray that you remove any feelings of insecurity that I possess. Thank you for looking out for me.

Prayer for Someone Else's Health

(Teacher, Friend or Relative)

Dear Father,

I pray for good health for my teacher, friend or relative. I pray that they have strength and courage in their life. I pray that they have the wisdom to see and make the correct choices regarding their health. I pray that they do not suffer. I pray for a speedy recovery. I pray for the wisdom to be able to see the lesson(s) in this situation and to grow from it in a positive way. Thank you for taking care of them and me.

Prayer to Combat Loneliness

Dear Lord,

I pray for the wisdom and strength to remove the loneliness that I feel inside. I pray for the wisdom to be able to see the lesson in this situation and to grow from it in a positive way. I pray for the awareness that my body is a reflection of your creation and that it is perfect in every way. I pray that you remove any feelings of insecurity that I may

possess. Thank you for blessing me.

Prayer to See the Beauty that Surrounds Us

Dear God,

I pray for the wisdom to be grateful no matter what my circumstances are. I pray for the wisdom to recognize my limitations and appreciate my progress. I pray for the wisdom to see the world differently and notice all the beauty that surrounds my life. Thank you for listening to me.

Prayer for Safety in Travels or Vacations

Dear Masters of the Universe,

I pray for the wisdom to make wise choices regarding my safety and the safety of others while traveling and/or on vacation. Thank you for taking care of me.

Prayer to Understand My Sexuality

Dear Goddess,

I pray for the wisdom to see and make the correct choices regarding my sexuality. I pray for the strength to stand up for my beliefs. I pray for the courage not to be bullied into a situation just to fit in. I pray that others will see me for the person that I am on the inside and that they will not judge me by my sexual preferences. I pray for the wisdom to love my body. I pray that you protect me from evil. I pray for the awareness that my body is a reflection of your creation and it is perfect in every way. I pray that you remove any feelings of insecurity that I possess. Thank you for looking out for me.

Prayer for Happiness

Dear Higher Power,

I pray that you will bless me and those around me with an abundance of happiness. Thank you for blessing me.

Prayer for Peace and Contentment without Worry

Dear Father,

I pray that you bless me with peace and contentment. I pray for the wisdom to remove all worry from my soul. I pray for the strength and courage to recognize contentment without worry. I pray that you remove any feelings of insecurity that I possess. Thank you for listening to me.

Prayer for Ending an Abusive Relationship

Dear Lord,

I pray for the wisdom, strength and courage to find a way out of my abusive relationship. I pray that you bless me with self-love. I pray for my safety. I pray for the strength to stand up for my beliefs and myself. I pray for the courage not to be bullied into a situation just to fit in. I pray for the wisdom to see and make the correct choices in my life. I pray for the wisdom to be able to see the lesson(s) in this situation and to grow from it in a positive way. I pray for the wisdom to love my body. I pray that you remove any feelings of insecurity that I may possess. Thank you for blessing me.

Prayer for Self-Esteem
and Self-Worth

Dear God,

I pray that you bless me with an abundance of self-esteem and self-worth. I pray for the wisdom to be able to distinguish self-destructive behavior from productive healthy behavior. I pray that I never forget my self-worth. I pray for the strength to stand up for my beliefs and myself. I pray for the courage not to be bullied into a bad situation just to fit in. I pray for the wisdom to love my body. I pray for the awareness that my body is a reflection of your creation and it is perfect in every way. Thank you for listening to me.

Prayer for Selflessness

Dear Masters of the Universe,

I pray for the wisdom to be selfless. I pray that I will be able to help others when needed and not expect anything from them. I am constantly reminded that the payback for selflessness is your blessings in my life. I pray that I am able to care for others from the goodness in my heart. I pray that I have the strength to stand up for my beliefs and myself. I pray for the courage not to be bullied into a bad situation just to fit in.

Thank you for blessing me.

Prayer to Overcome Hate and Anxiety

Dear Goddess,

I pray for the wisdom, courage and strength to remove the hate that I feel for another individual. I pray for the wisdom to replace these feelings of hate and anxiety with feelings of compassion and understanding. I pray for the strength to stand up for my beliefs and myself. I pray for the courage not to be bullied into a bad situation just to fit in. I pray for the wisdom to be able to see the lesson in this situation and to grow from it in a positive way. I pray that you remove any feelings of insecurity that I possess. Thank you for taking care of me.

Prayer to Overcome Panic Attacks

Dear Higher Power,

I pray for the wisdom, strength and courage to overcome my panic attacks. I pray for the wisdom to be able to see the lessons in this situation and to grow from it in a positive way. I pray for the wisdom to love my body. I pray for the awareness that my body is a reflection of your creation and it is perfect in every way. I pray that you remove any feelings of insecurity that I possess. Thank you for blessing me.

Prayer to Tell the Truth and Not a Lie

Dear Father,

I pray for the wisdom, strength and courage to tell the truth and not lie. I pray that I will have the courage to stand up for my beliefs and myself and not be bullied into a bad situation just to fit in. Thank you for listening to me.

Prayer to Forgive Someone

Dear Lord,

I pray for the wisdom, strength, courage and compassion to forgive the individual who I feel has betrayed me. I pray for the wisdom to see and make the correct choices in this situation. I pray for the courage to stand up for my beliefs and myself and not to be bullied into a bad situation just to fit in. I pray for the wisdom to be able to see the lesson in this situation and to grow from it in a positive way. Thank you for blessing me.

Prayer to End Confusion

Dear God,

I am confused and do not know what decision is the correct decision. I pray for a sign that will show me which decision is the correct decision. I pray for the wisdom that I will recognize the sign when presented to me. I pray for the courage to stand up for my beliefs and myself and not to be bullied into a bad situation just to fit in. I pray for the wisdom to be able to see the lesson in this situation and to grow from it in a positive way. Thank you for looking out for me.

Prayer for Creativity

Dear Masters of the Universe,

I pray for patience to participate in the creative process. I pray for the wisdom to recognize the creative signs that are being shown to me. Thank you for taking care of me.

Prayer for Living with Divorced Parents

Dear Goddess,

I pray that you will bless both of my parents and guide them with the wisdom to see and make wise choices regarding our family. I pray that you remove hurt, hate or unhealthy feelings from my family. I pray that you bless us with an abundance of understanding. I pray for the wisdom to be able to see the lesson in this situation and to grow from it in a positive way. I pray that you remove any feelings of insecurity that I possess. Thank you for blessing me.

Prayer for New Home and Neighborhood

Dear Higher Power,

I pray that you will bless our new home and neighborhood. I pray for the safety of my family in our new home and neighborhood. I pray that you will bless us with an abundance of happy memories in our new home and neighborhood. I pray that you remove any feelings of insecurity that I possess. Thank you for taking care of me.

Prayer for New School

Dear Father,

I pray that you will remove any fear or anxiety about attending my new school. I pray that you will protect me from all harm and evil people. I pray for the wisdom to make friends. I pray for the courage to stand up for my beliefs and not to be bullied into a bad situation just to fit in. I pray for the wisdom to love my body. I pray for the awareness that my body is a reflection of your creation and it is perfect in every way. I pray for the wisdom to learn what is being taught to me. I pray that you remove any feelings of insecurity that I possess. Thank you for listening to me.

Prayer for the Wisdom to See and Make the Correct Choice

Dear Lord,

I pray for the wisdom to see and make wise choices in all areas of my life. I pray for the wisdom to be able to see the lessons necessary for me to learn and to grow from them in a positive way. I pray that you remove any feelings of insecurity that I possess. Thank you for blessing me.

Prayer for Sports

Dear God,

I pray for the wisdom to perfect my skills and talents regarding my favorite sports. I pray for the wisdom to be aware of the opportunities to become better at my favorite sports. I pray for the safety and the safety of others while I am participating in my favorite sports. I pray that you will remove any feelings of insecurity that I possess. Thank you for taking care of me.

Prayer for Love

Dear Masters of the Universe,

I pray to be blessed with unconditional love. I pray for the wisdom to love others unconditionally. Thank you for taking care of me.

Prayer to Be True to Yourself

Dear Goddess,

I pray for the courage to stand up for my beliefs and myself and not to be bullied into a bad situation just to fit in. I pray for the wisdom to love my body. I pray that you remove any feelings of insecurity that I possess. Thank you for looking out for me.

Prayer to Battle Bad Eating Habits

Dear Higher Power,

I pray for the wisdom to be able to identify bad eating habits from healthy eating habits. I pray for the strength and courage to make the correct decisions regarding my weight. I pray that others will not judge me because of my weight and that they will see me for the great person that I am on the inside. I pray for good health. I pray for the wisdom to be able to see the lesson in this situation and to grow from it in a positive way. I pray for the wisdom to love my body. I pray that you remove any feelings of insecurity that I posses. Thank you for blessing me.

Prayer for Developing
a Sense of Style

Dear Father,

I pray for the wisdom to remember that I am an unique. I pray for the courage to be able to develop my own look. I pray for the strength to be able to stay with what works best for me, no matter what everyone else is wearing. I pray that you remove any feelings of insecurity that I possess. Thank you for taking care of me.

Prayer for Your Hair

Dear Lord,

I pray for the wisdom to accept that loving my
hair is part of the process of loving myself. I
pray that I am reminded that my hair is a living,
powerful, energy force. I pray for the wisdom to
work with my hair and not to fight it. I pray
that you remove any feelings of insecurity that I
possess. Thank you for taking care of me.

Prayer to Pass a Test

Dear God,

I pray for the wisdom to remember all the things that I have been taught. I pray for the wisdom to remove any anxiety or confusion. I pray for confidence in my abilities. I pray that you remove any feelings of insecurity that I possess. Thank you for taking care of me.

Prayer to Get the Message

Dear Masters of the Universe,

I pray for the wisdom to learn what I am suppose to learn during my time here on earth. I pray that I will be guided and protected as I walk through life. I pray for the wisdom to see the daily miracles that are so graciously sprinkled in my life. Thank you for listening to me.

Prayer to Live in the Moment

Dear Goddess,

I pray for the wisdom to be aware, each and every day, of my special life. I pray for the wisdom to not take anything for granted and to be gracious for the gift of life. Thank you for blessing to me.

Prayer for Addictions

(Gambling, Anorexia, Bulimia, Drugs, Alcohol, Smoking, Sex, Food, Spending)

Dear Higher Power,

I pray for the wisdom, strength and courage to recognize things in my life that will help me overcome my addiction. I pray for the wisdom to make the correct choices. I pray for the strength and courage to stand up for my beliefs and myself and not to be bullied into a bad situation just to fit in. I pray for the wisdom to be able to see the lesson in this situation and to grow from it in a positive way. I pray for the wisdom to love my body. I pray for the awareness that my body is perfect in every way. I pray that you remove any feelings of insecurity that I possess. Thank you for listening to me.

Prayer Because I am Being Bullied

Dear Father,

I pray for the courage and strength to stand up for my beliefs and myself and not to be bullied into a bad situation just to fit in. I pray that you will remove any fear or anxiety from me. I pray that you will protect me from all harm and evil people. I pray for the wisdom to be able to forgive the person who has bullied me. I understand that hate and resentment are not positive and I pray for the wisdom to remove it. I pray for the wisdom to be able to see the lesson in this situation and to grow from it in a positive way. Thank you for looking out for me.

Prayer to Release Fear

Dear Lord,

I pray that you remove these scary feelings that I possess. I pray that you bless me with peace and contentment. Thank you for taking care of me.

Prayer for a Birthday

Dear God,

I thank you for another year of life. I thank you for another 365 opportunities to learn life's lessons. Thank you for taking care of me.

Prayer for Before the Prom

Dear Masters of the Universe,

I pray that I am directed to be asked or to ask the right person to attend the prom with me. I pray for my safety and the safety of my date at the prom. I pray for the wisdom to make the correct choices on prom night. I pray for the wisdom to be able to identify bad choices. I pray for the courage and strength to stand up for my beliefs and not to be bullied into a bad situation just to fit in. I pray that I have a great time and create wonderful memories. I pray that you remove any feelings of insecurity that I possess. Thank you for looking out for me.

Prayer to Lose Weight

Dear Goddess,

I pray for the wisdom to make the food choices that benefit my body the most. I pray for the strength and courage to say no to unhealthy food choices. I pray for the wisdom to love my body. I pray for the awareness that my body is perfect in every way. I pray that you remove any insecurity that I possess. Thank you for blessing me.

Prayer for Family and Friends

Dear Higher Power,

Thank you for the friends that I have in my life. Thank you for my parents, brothers, sisters, nieces, nephews, grandparents, aunts, uncles and friends. I pray that you will bless and watch over each and every one of them. Thank you for listening to me.

Prayer for Forgiveness

Dear Father,

I pray for forgiveness. I acted wrongly and am
very sorry. Thank you for listening to me.

Prayer for Step-Family

Dear Lord,

I pray for the wisdom to love and accept my step-family. I pray that my step-family will love and accept me. I pray for the wisdom to learn the lesson that I am suppose to learn in this situation and to grow from it in a positive way. I pray that you remove any insecurity that I possess. Thank you for listening to me.

Prayer Get the Most Out of My Education

Dear God,

I pray for the wisdom and guidance to use my education to everyone's benefit. I pray for the wisdom to see opportunities when presented to me regarding my education Thank you for blessing me.

Prayer to Listen

Dear Masters of the Universe,

I pray for the strength and courage to stop talking and begin listening more. I pray for the courage to stand up for my beliefs. I pray for the wisdom to learn the lesson that I am suppose to learn in this situation and to grow from it in a positive way. I pray that you remove any insecurity that I possess. Thank you for taking care of me.

Prayer to End Bed-wetting

Dear Goddess,

I pray for the wisdom, strength and courage to conquer bed-wetting. I pray that others will not judge me because of my bed-wetting and that they will see me for the great person I am on the inside. I pray for the wisdom to be able to see the lesson in this situation and to grow from it in a positive way. I pray for the wisdom to love my body. I pray for the awareness that my body is a reflection of your creation and it is perfect in every way. I pray that you remove any insecurity that I possess. Thank you for listening to me.

Prayer to Distance Myself from Gang Involvement

Dear Higher Power,

I pray for the wisdom to see what gang involvement really means and does to families. I pray for my safety and the safety of my family. I pray for the wisdom to see the opportunities to distance myself from gang involvement. I pray for the strength and courage to stand up for my beliefs and not to be bullied into a situation just to fit in. I pray for the wisdom to be able to see the lesson in this and grow from it in a positive way. Thank you for protecting me.

Prayer to Get a Wage or Allowance Increase

Dear Father,

I pray to get a wage increase or allowance increase. I pray that if this is not meant for me to have that I will have the wisdom to see why. I pray for the strength to have patience to wait for the opportunity to obtain my wage or allowance increase. I pray for the wisdom to be able to see the lesson in this. Thank you for taking care of me.

Prayer for Patience in Waiting my Turn

Dear Lord,

I pray for the wisdom to see the benefit of waiting my turn. I pray for the strength and courage to be able to wait my turn. I pray for the wisdom to be able to see the lesson in this situation and to grow from it in a positive way. Thank you for taking care of me.

Prayer to Make the Most of My Talent

Dear God,

I pray for the wisdom to be able to identify opportunities that are presented to me where I can use my talents. I pray that you remove any feelings of insecurity that I possess. Thank you for listening to me.

Prayer to Overcome Stage Fright

Dear Masters of the Universe,

I pray for the strength and courage to overcome my stage fright. I pray that others will not judge me while I am on stage and that they will see me for the great person that I am. I pray for the wisdom to love my body. I pray for the awareness that my body is a reflection of your creation and that it is perfect in every way. I pray that you remove any feelings of insecurity that I possess. Thank you for blessing me.

Prayer to Accept Blame and Not Blame Others

Dear Goddess,

I pray for the strength and courage to accept blame for my mistakes. I pray for the wisdom to be responsible for my actions and not to place blame on others. I pray for the wisdom to learn the lessons in this situation. Thank you for taking care of me.

Prayer When Breaking Up

Dear Higher Power,

I pray for the strength and courage to distance myself from this guy/girl. I pray for the wisdom to see and understand why this relationship is not beneficial to me. I pray for the strength and courage to stand up for my beliefs and not be bullied into a situation just to fit in. I pray that you remove any insecurity that I possess. Thank you for blessing me.

Prayer to Eliminate Jealousy

Dear Father,

I pray for the wisdom, strength and courage to overcome my jealousy. I pray for the wisdom to see how this behavior is not beneficial to me or anyone else. I pray for the strength and courage not to be bullied into a bad situation just to fit in. Thank you for blessing me.

Prayer to Accept a Compliment

Dear Lord,

I pray for the wisdom to be able to accept a compliment. I pray for the wisdom to love myself and my talents. I pray for the awareness that my talents are a reflection of your creation and that they are perfect in every way. I pray that you remove any insecurity that I may possess. Thank you for listening.

Prayer for Abstinence

Dear God,

I pray for the wisdom, strength and courage to be able to refrain from indulging in alcohol, drugs and sex. I pray for the strength to stand up for my beliefs and myself. I pray for the courage to not be bullied into a bad situation just to fit in. I pray for the wisdom to be able to see how abstinence is beneficial to me and others. I pray that you remove any insecurity I may possess. Thank you for blessing me.

Prayer to Read Faster

Dear Masters of the Universe,

I pray for the wisdom to be able to read faster. I pray for the wisdom to be able to retain what I read. I pray that you remove any insecurity that I may possess. Thank you for listening to me.

Prayer to Wake Up On Time

Dear Goddess,

I pray for the wisdom, strength and courage to be able to wake up on time. I pray for the wisdom to go to bed at a decent hour. I pray for the wisdom to take care of myself and get adequate rest. Thank you for taking care of me.

Prayer to Exercise Regularly

Dear Higher Power,

I pray for the wisdom, strength and courage to exercise regularly. I pray for the wisdom to be able to recognize the benefits. I pray for the wisdom to love my body. I pray for the awareness that my body is a reflection of your creation and it is perfect in every way. I pray that you remove any feelings of insecurity I possess. Thank you for blessing me.

Prayer to Speak Up

Dear Father,

I pray for the wisdom, courage and strength to speak up for myself. I pray for the wisdom to be able to recognize the benefits of speaking up for myself. I pray for strength and courage to stand up for myself and my beliefs and not to be bullied into any situation just to fit in. I pray that you remove any feelings of insecurity that I may possess. Thank you for taking care of me.

Prayer to Overcome Sneaky Behavior

Dear Lord,

I pray for the wisdom, strength and courage to overcome my sneaky behavior. I pray for the wisdom to be able to see that this behavior is not healthy or beneficial to me or others. I pray for the strength and courage to stand up for my beliefs and myself. I pray for the courage not to be bullied into a bad situation just to fit in.

Thank you for blessing me.

Prayer to Love my Body

Dear God,

I pray for the wisdom, strength and courage to love my body. I pray for the strength and courage to stand up for my beliefs and myself and not to be bullied into a bad situation just to fit in. I pray for the awareness that my body is a reflection of your creation and it is perfect in every way. I pray that you remove any feelings of insecurity that I possess. Thank you for looking out for me.

Prayer to Overcome a Spending Addiction

Dear Masters of the Universe,

I pray for the wisdom to understand my spending addiction. I pray for the strength and courage to overcome my spending addition. Thank you for blessing me.

Prayer for Heroic Behavior

Dear Goddess,

I pray for the strength, courage and wisdom to be the hero in this situation. I pray to be blessed with the wisdom to be able to identify the right course of action. I pray that you remove any insecurity that I possess. Thank you for listening to me.

Prayer for Getting a Pet

Dear Father,

I pray for the wisdom to understand the responsibility that goes into owning a pet. I pray for the strength and courage to show my parents that I am ready to make a commitment to a pet. If this isn't the time for me to have a pet I pray for the wisdom to see the reasons why. Thank you for blessing me.

Prayer for Safety on the Internet

Dear Lord,

I pray for my safety and the safety of my friends on the internet. I pray for the wisdom to make the correct choices when using the internet. I pray for the strength and courage to not be bullied into a bad situation just to fit in.

Thank you for listening to me.

My Personalized Prayers

PRAYER FOR/TO

.

www.ingramcontent.com/pod-product-compliance
Lightning Source LLC
Chambersburg PA
CBHW032015040426

42448CB00006B/641